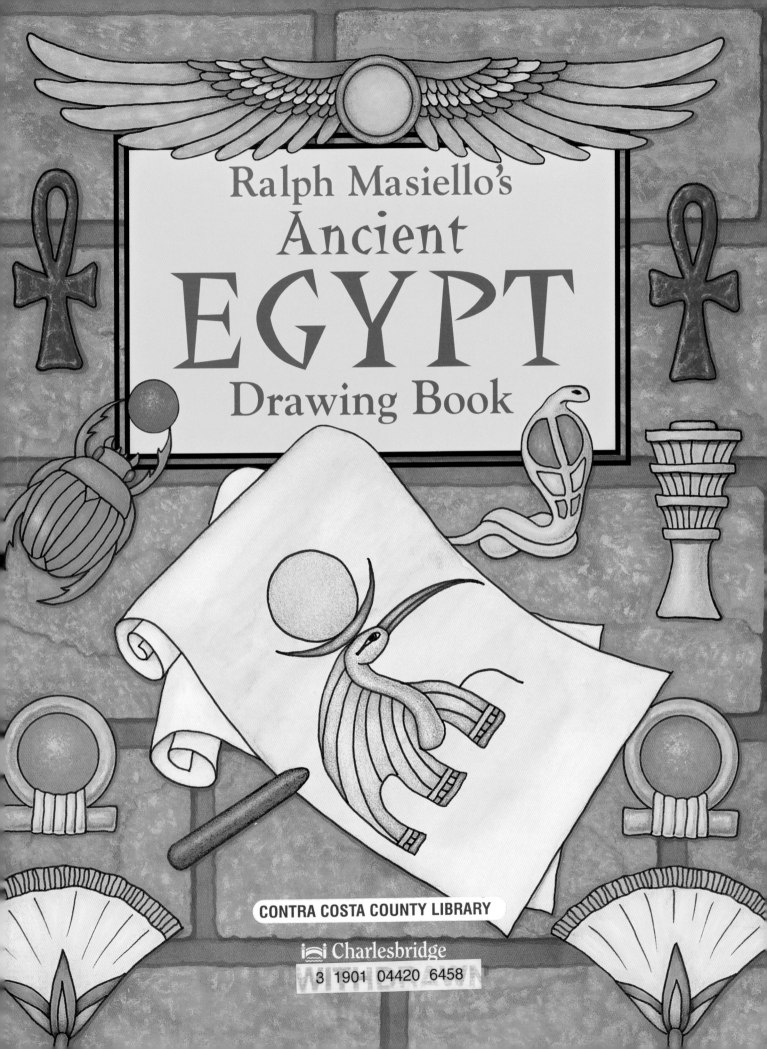

Ralph Masiello's
Ancient
EGYPT
Drawing Book

Charlesbridge

For my nephew, Zachary, who thinks I'm famous—R. M.

Also in this series:

Ralph Masiello's Bug Drawing Book

Ralph Masiello's Dinosaur Drawing Book

Ralph Masiello's Dragon Drawing Book

Ralph Masiello's Ocean Drawing Book

Other books illustrated by Ralph Masiello:

The Dinosaur Alphabet Book

The Extinct Alphabet Book

The Flag We Love

The Frog Alphabet Book

The Icky Bug Alphabet Book

The Icky Bug Counting Book

The Skull Alphabet Book

The Yucky Reptile Alphabet Book

Cuenta los insectos

Published by Charlesbridge
85 Main Street
Watertown, MA 02472
(617) 926-0329
www.charlesbridge.com

Library of Congress Cataloging-in-Publication Data
Masiello, Ralph.
    Ralph Masiello's ancient Egypt drawing book.
        p. cm.
    Includes bibliographical references.
    ISBN 978-1-57091-533-8 (reinforced for library use)
    ISBN 978-1-57091-534-5 (softcover)
1. Egypt—In art—Juvenile literature. 2. Egypt—Civilization—To 332 B.C.—Juvenile literature. 3. Drawing—Technique—Juvenile literature. I. Title. II. Title: Ancient Egypt drawing book.
NC825.E38M37 2008
743'.89932—dc22   2007027023

Printed in China
(hc) 10 9 8 7 6 5 4 3 2 1
(sc) 10 9 8 7 6 5 4 3 2 1

Illustrations done in mixed media
Display type and text type set in La Bamba and Goudy
Color separations by Chroma Graphics, Singapore
Printed and bound by Jade Productions
Production supervision by Brian G. Walker
Designed by Susan Mallory Sherman and Martha MacLeod Sikkema

Hello, Fellow Artists!

Some five thousand years ago in northeast Africa, along the fertile upper Nile River Valley, an incredible civilization emerged. Ancient Egypt was a place of pharaohs, of gods and goddesses, of temples and tombs. It was also a time of great human achievement. The Egyptians developed an incredibly complex system of writing and made important advancements in math and science. They also developed wonderfully stylized art forms and built architecture that has survived for thousands of years.

Even today, as archaeologists try to unlock the mysteries of Ancient Egypt, the wonder of that vast culture looms in our imaginations. In this book I'll show you some of the Egyptian images and symbols that I think are the most interesting to draw. Follow the steps in red to draw these images. Then color in your drawings with your favorite art tools. Extra challenge steps in blue show how to add details to your Ancient Egyptian creations.

Have fun, practice, and keep on drawing! (And go to the library to learn more about this fascinating civilization.)

Ralph

Choose your tools

pastel pencil | crayon | watercolor | fine-tip marker | colored pencil | marker | poster paint

— Great Pyramid of Khafre —

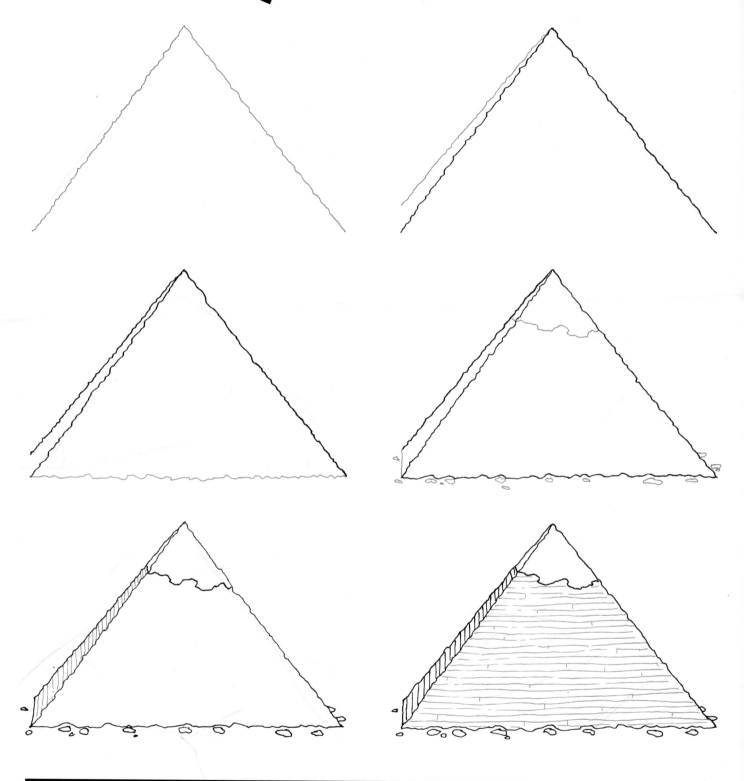

Sun, Horizon, and Clouds

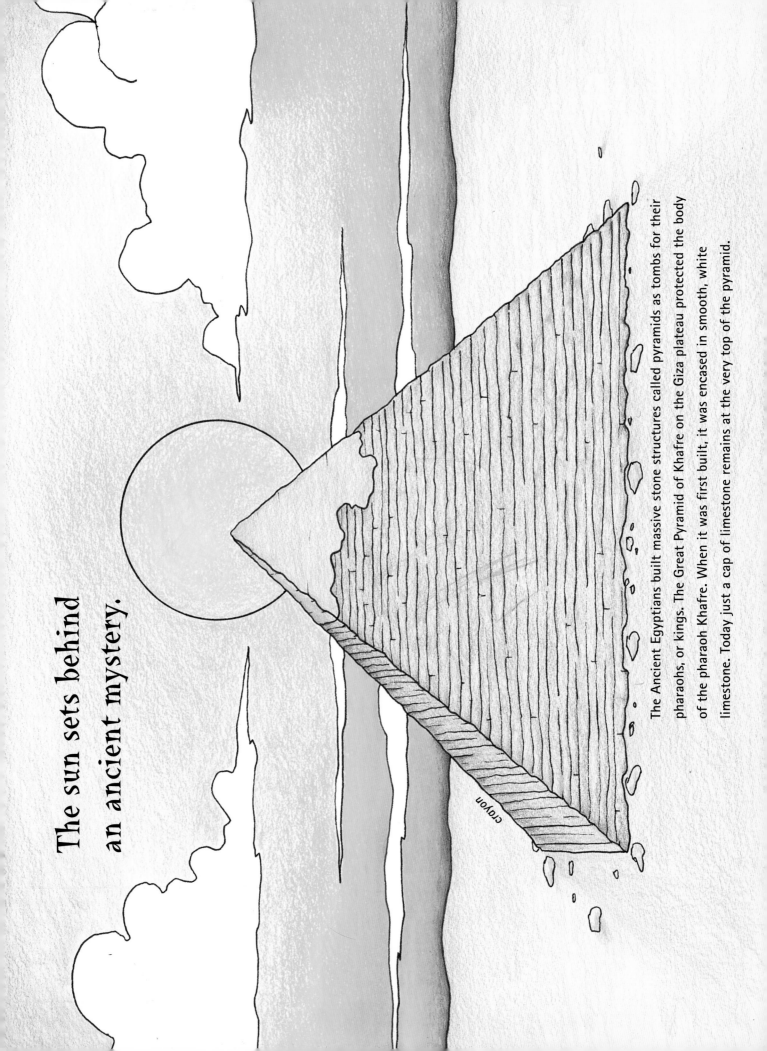

The sun sets behind
an ancient mystery.

The Ancient Egyptians built massive stone structures called pyramids as tombs for their pharaohs, or kings. The Great Pyramid of Khafre on the Giza plateau protected the body of the pharaoh Khafre. When it was first built, it was encased in smooth, white limestone. Today just a cap of limestone remains at the very top of the pyramid.

crayon

—The Udjat, or Eye of Horus—

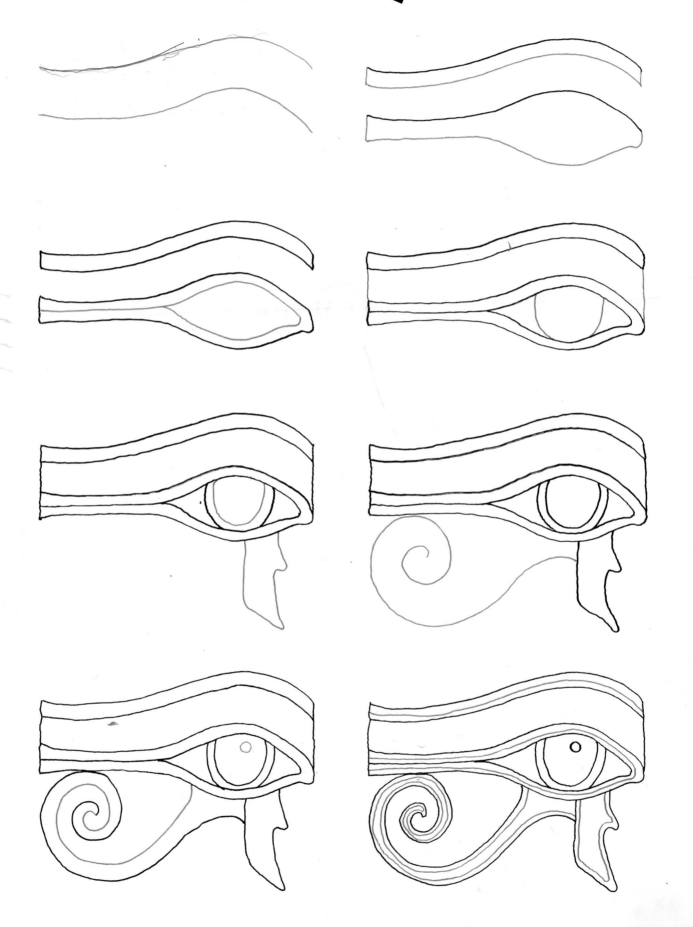

There's more to drawing than meets the eye.

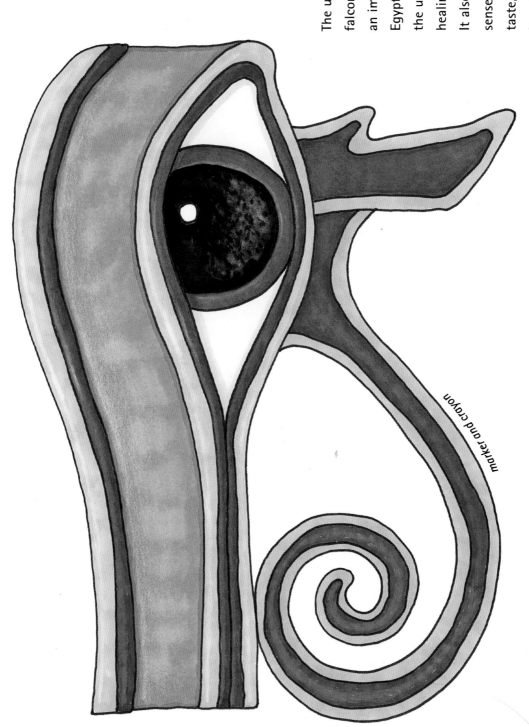

marker and crayon

The udjat, the right eye of the falcon-headed god, Horus, was an important symbol in Ancient Egypt. Associated with the sun, the udjat was thought to have healing and magical powers. It also represented the five senses of touch, hearing, smell, taste, and sight. The left eye, its mirror image, was associated with the moon and with the ibis-headed god, Thoth.

Symbols and Emblems of Ancient Egypt

Shen Ring: Symbol of eternity and strength

Ankh: Symbol of life

Djed Pillar (bundle of reeds): Symbol of rebirth and stability, and the emblem of Osiris, god of the dead

Uraeus (rearing cobra): Symbol of the sun, Lower Egypt, pharaohs, and many deities

Scarab: Symbol of transformation, resurrection, and the rising of the sun

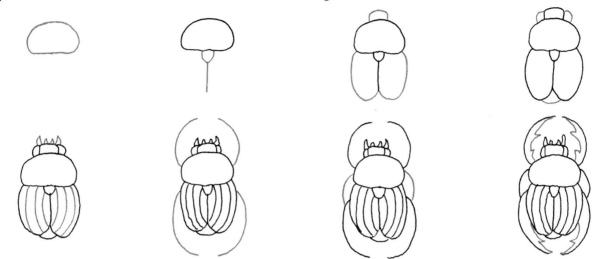

Blue Lotus: Symbol of the sun and creation, as well as symbol of Upper Egypt

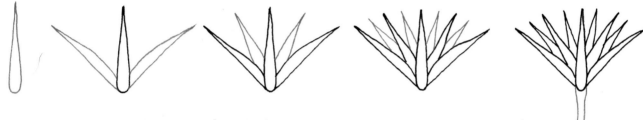

Papyrus: Symbol of life itself, as well as symbol of Lower Egypt

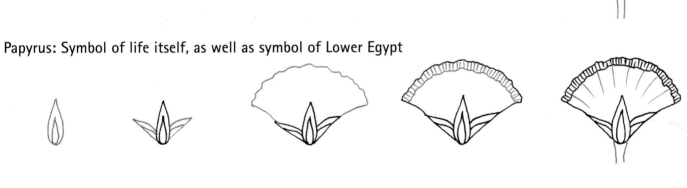

Crook and Flail: Symbols of the pharaoh's rule

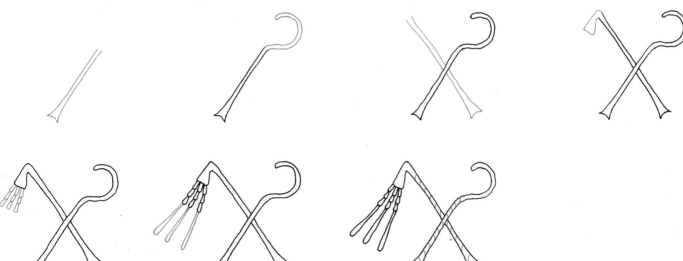

Nekhbet (vulture): Goddess protector of pharaohs, and symbol of Upper Egypt

Was-Scepter: Symbol of power and dominion

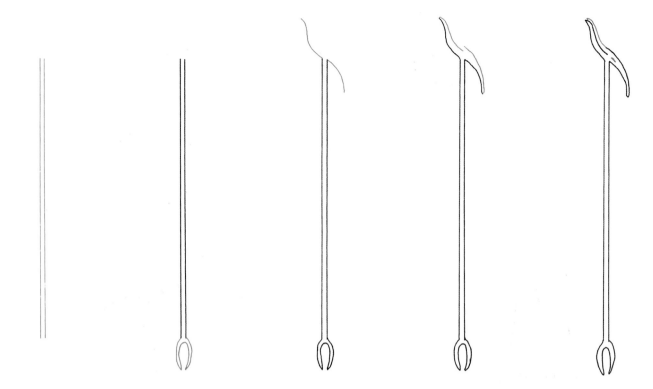

Deshret or Red Crown: Symbol of Lower Egypt

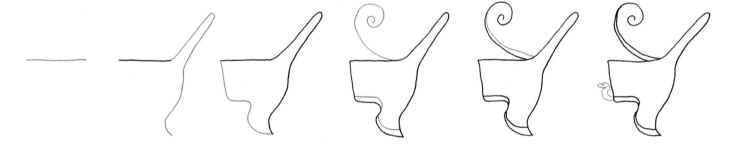

Pshent or Double Crown: Symbol of unified Upper and Lower Egypt

Hedjet or White Crown: Symbol of Upper Egypt

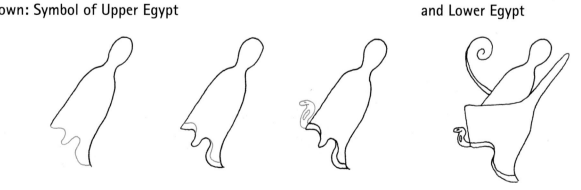

The deshret and the hedjet (both adorned with cobras) were combined to form the pshent or double crown.

Winged Solar Disk

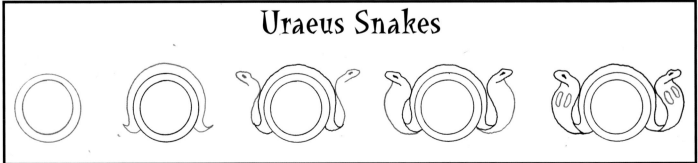

Uraeus Snakes

Add some ancient symbols to your winged wonder.

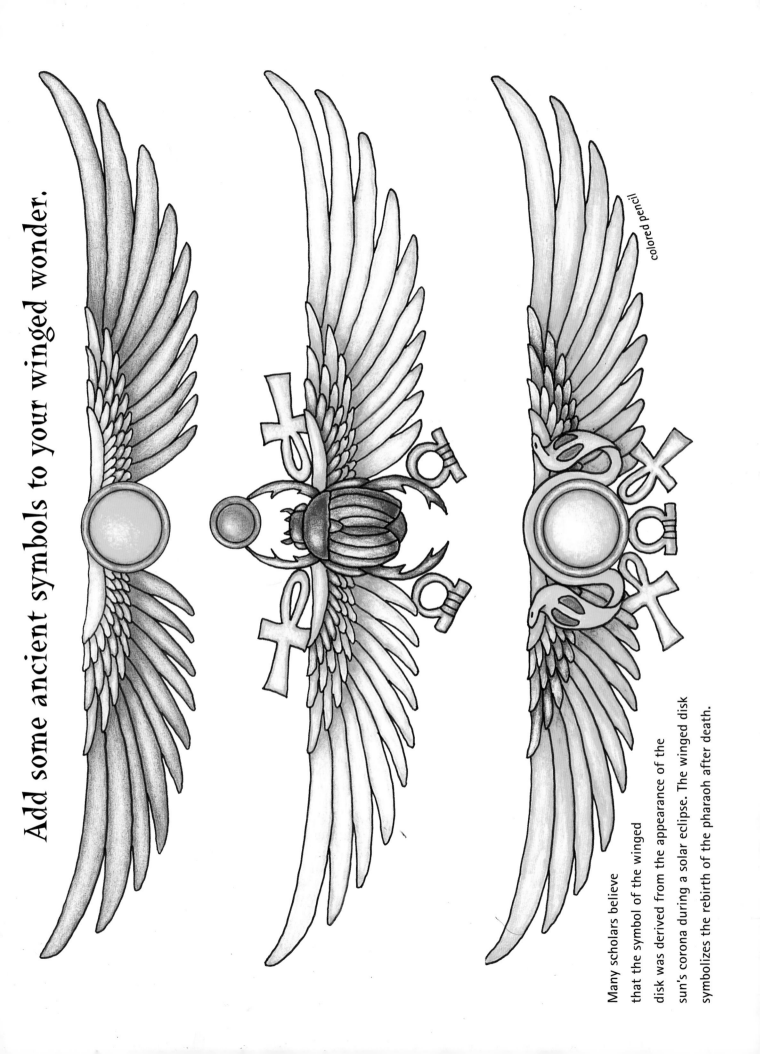

colored pencil

Many scholars believe
that the symbol of the winged
disk was derived from the appearance of the
sun's corona during a solar eclipse. The winged disk
symbolizes the rebirth of the pharaoh after death.

Anubis, God of the Dead

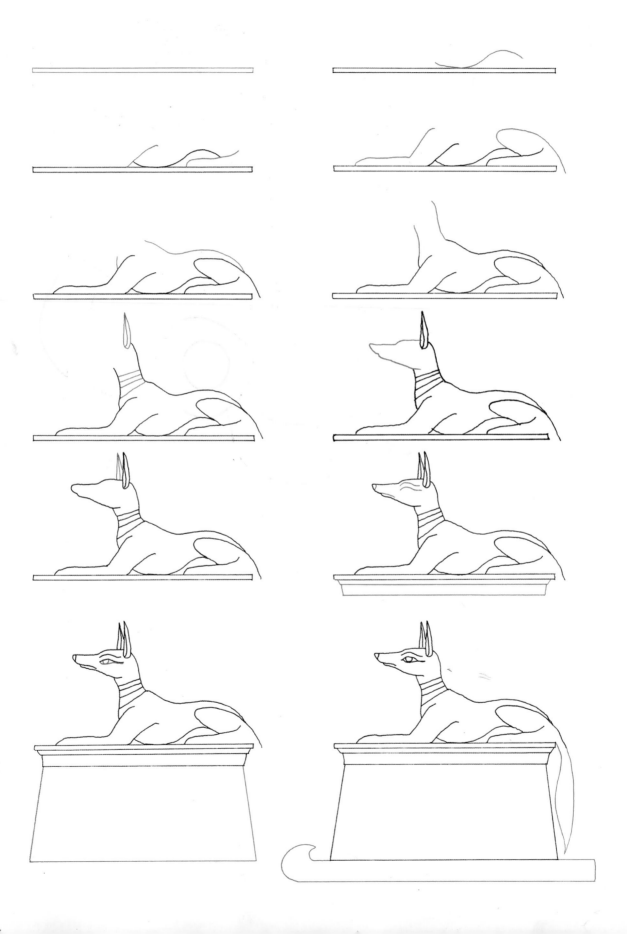

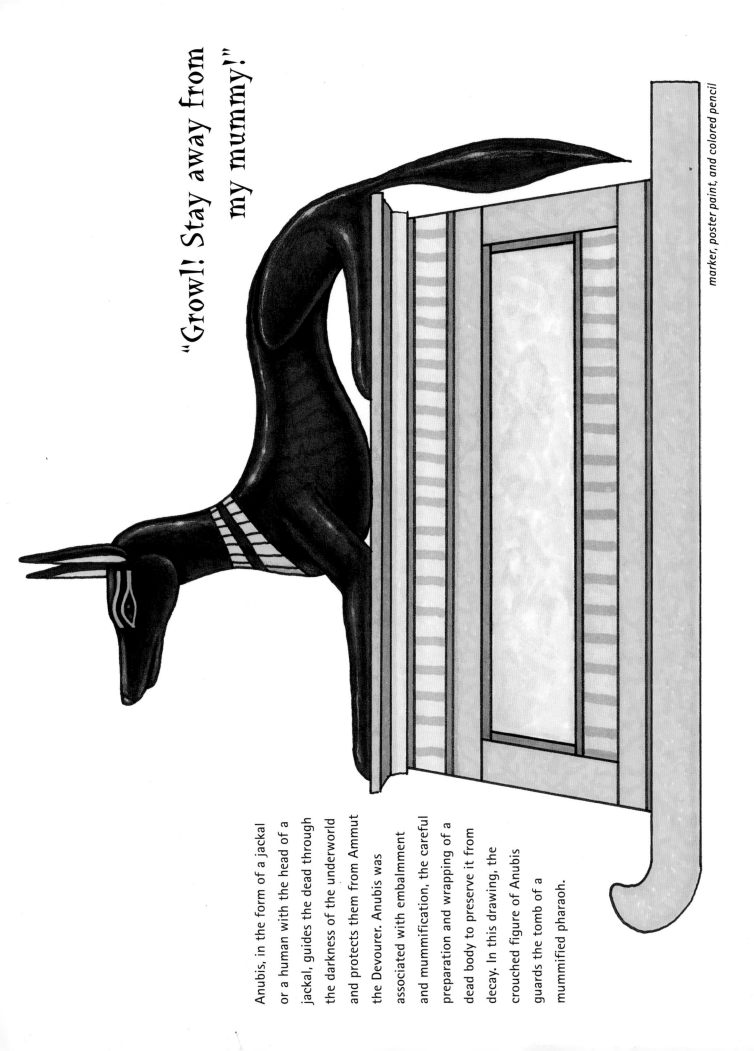

"Growl! Stay away from my mummy!"

marker, poster paint, and colored pencil

Anubis, in the form of a jackal or a human with the head of a jackal, guides the dead through the darkness of the underworld and protects them from Ammut the Devourer. Anubis was associated with embalmment and mummification, the careful preparation and wrapping of a dead body to preserve it from decay. In this drawing, the crouched figure of Anubis guards the tomb of a mummified pharaoh.

Sphinx Body

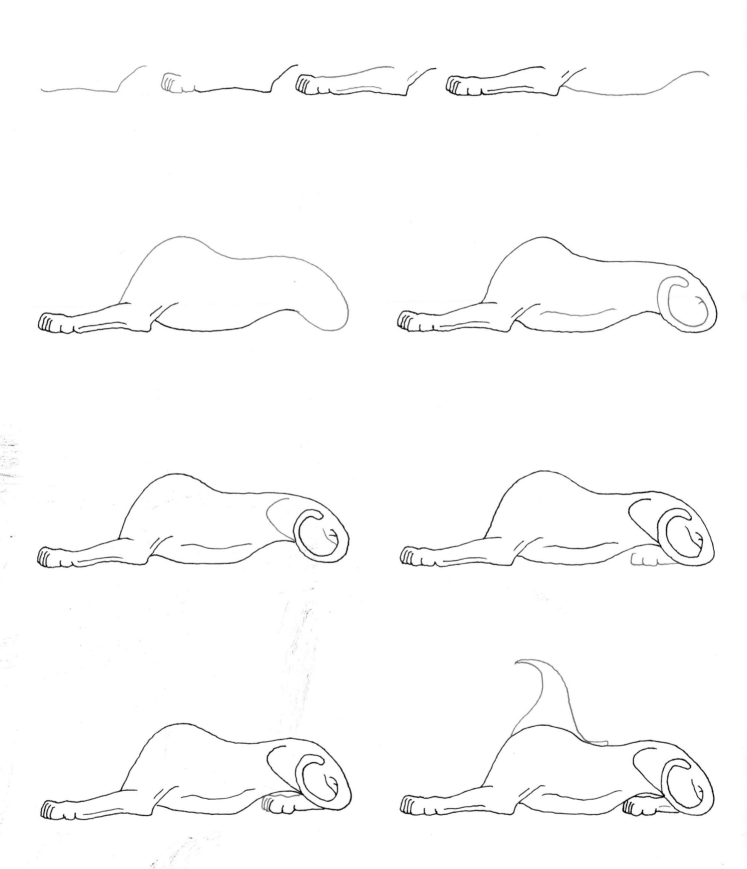

Kriosphinx Head

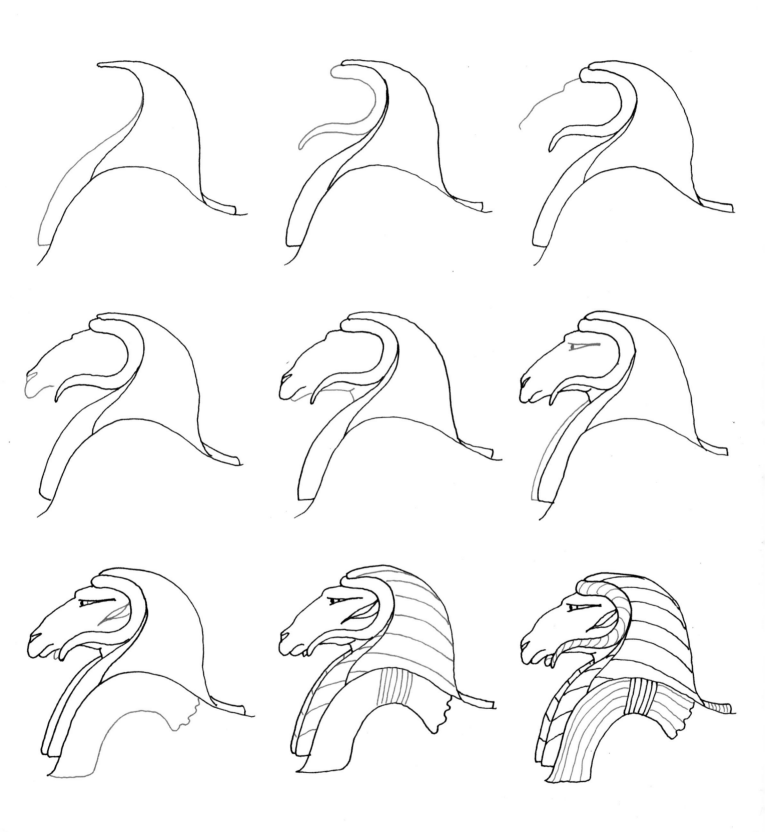

Hieracosphinx Head

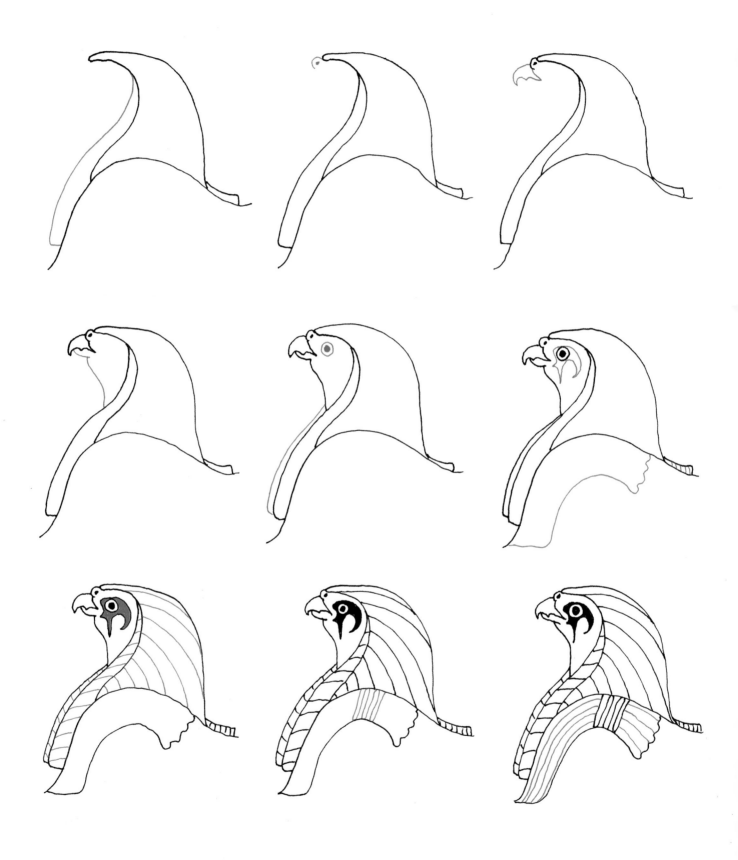

Androsphinx Head

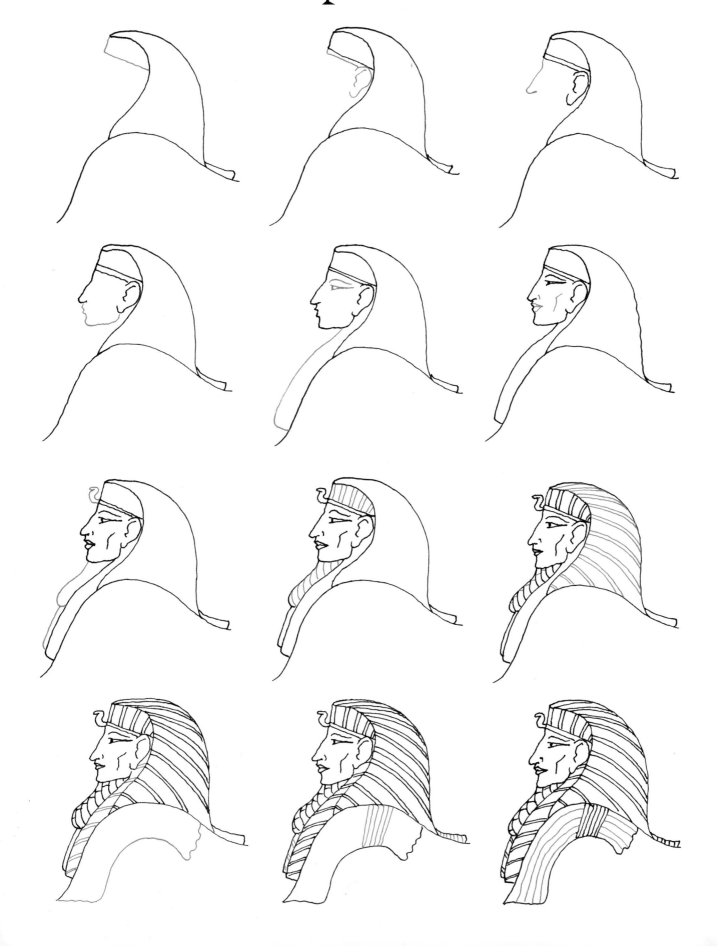

This drawing really "sphinx"!

An androsphinx has the
body of a lion with the
head of a god or pharaoh.

A hieracosphinx has the
body of a lion with the
head of a falcon or hawk.

watercolor and marker

A kriosphinx has the body of a lion with the head of a ram.

Osiris, God of the Dead and First Mummy of Egypt

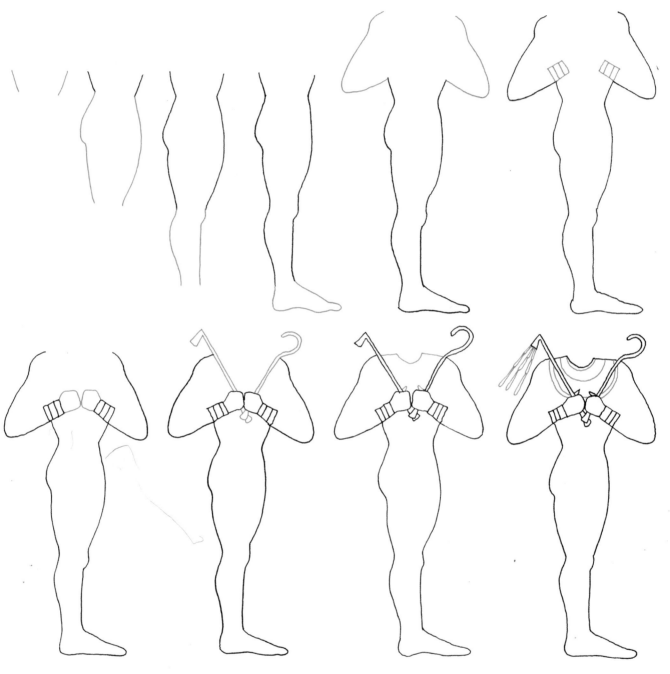

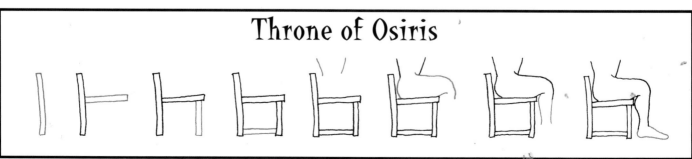

Throne of Osiris

Head of Osiris

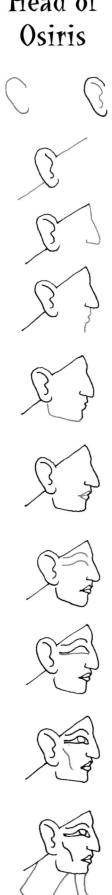

Osiris sits in judgment of the dead.

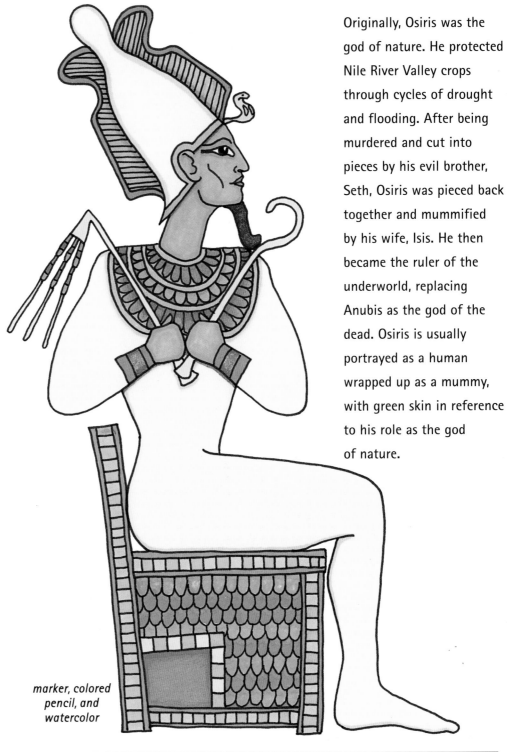

Originally, Osiris was the god of nature. He protected Nile River Valley crops through cycles of drought and flooding. After being murdered and cut into pieces by his evil brother, Seth, Osiris was pieced back together and mummified by his wife, Isis. He then became the ruler of the underworld, replacing Anubis as the god of the dead. Osiris is usually portrayed as a human wrapped up as a mummy, with green skin in reference to his role as the god of nature.

marker, colored pencil, and watercolor

Feathered Crown of Osiris

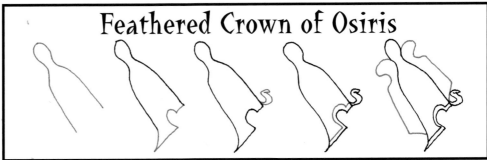

Ancient Egyptian Gods

Thoth: God of wisdom and writing

Seth or Set: God of chaos and evil

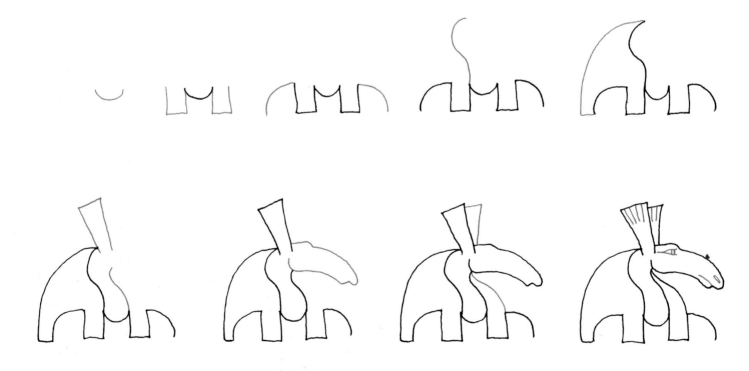

Anubis: God of the dead

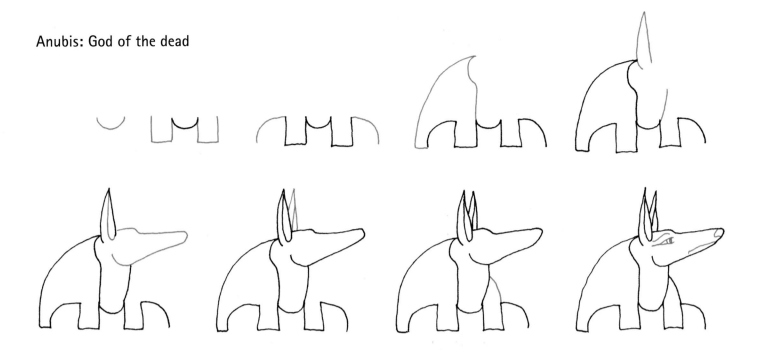

Sobek: Crocodile god of water and guardian of other gods and pharaohs

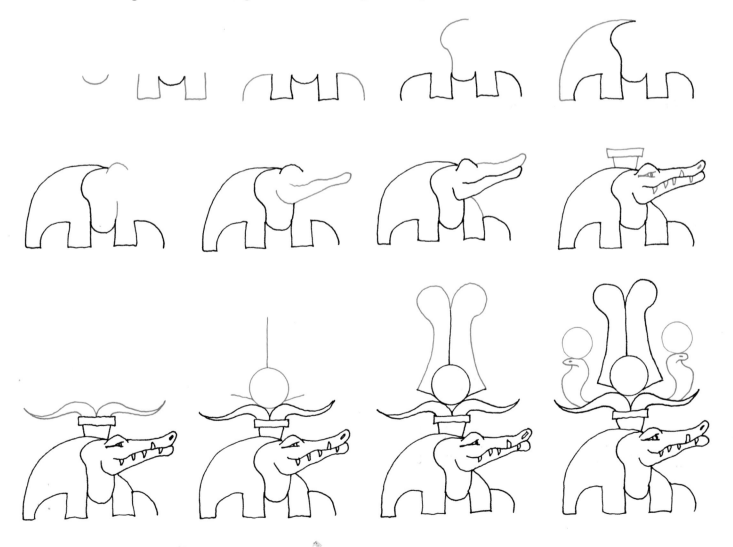

Horus: God of the sky and king of the gods on earth

Ra or Re: Sun god and father of the gods

The god Ra or Re has a falcon head like Horus but wears a sun headdress.

Body of a God

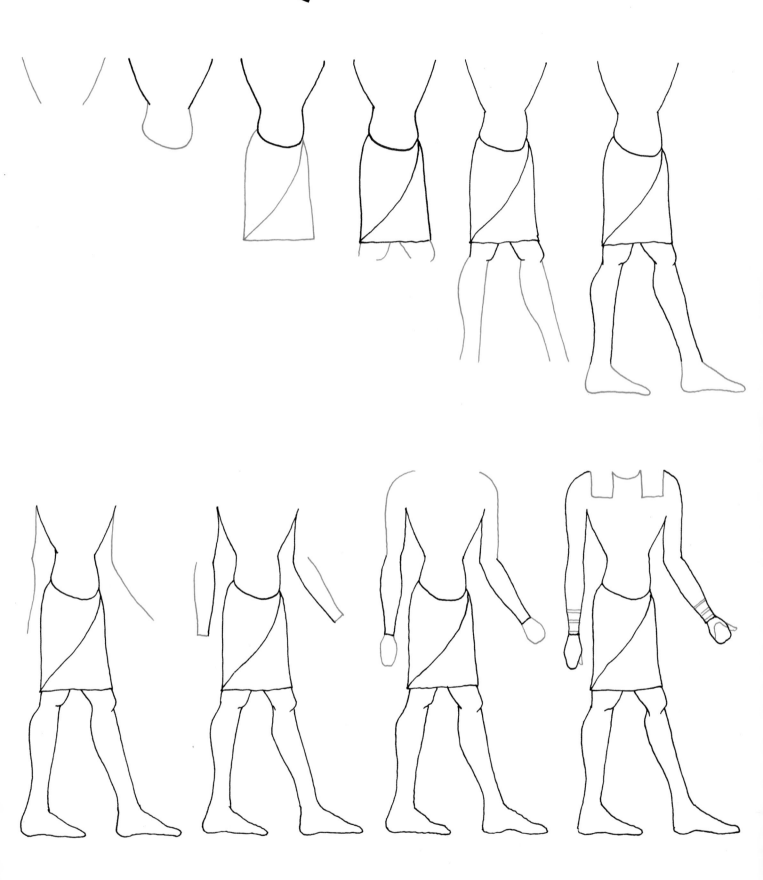

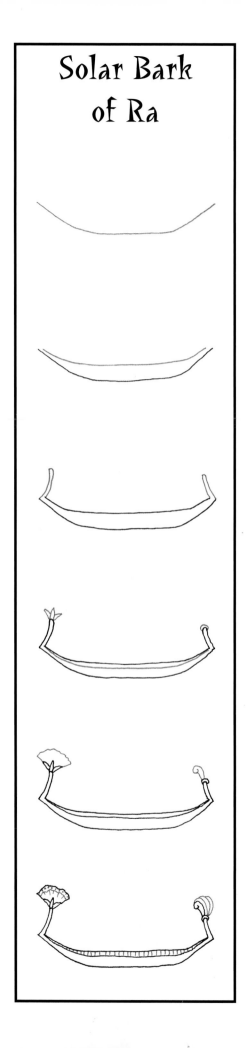

Solar Bark of Ra

The sun god, Ra, accompanied by the crocodile god, Sobek, slips across the horizon.

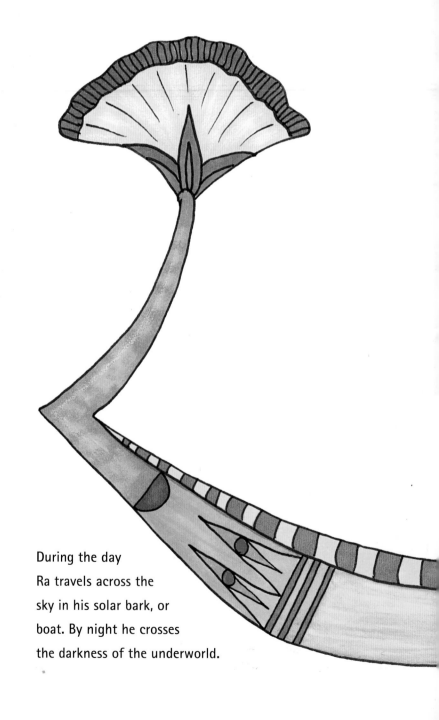

During the day Ra travels across the sky in his solar bark, or boat. By night he crosses the darkness of the underworld.

marker, watercolor, colored pencil, and poster paint

Isis, Queen of the Gods

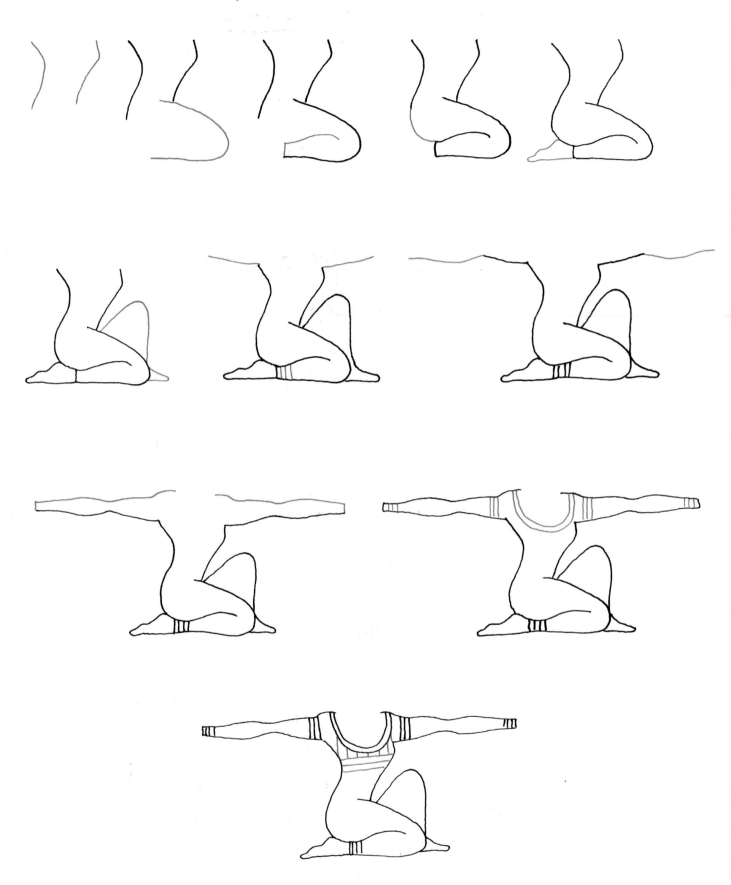

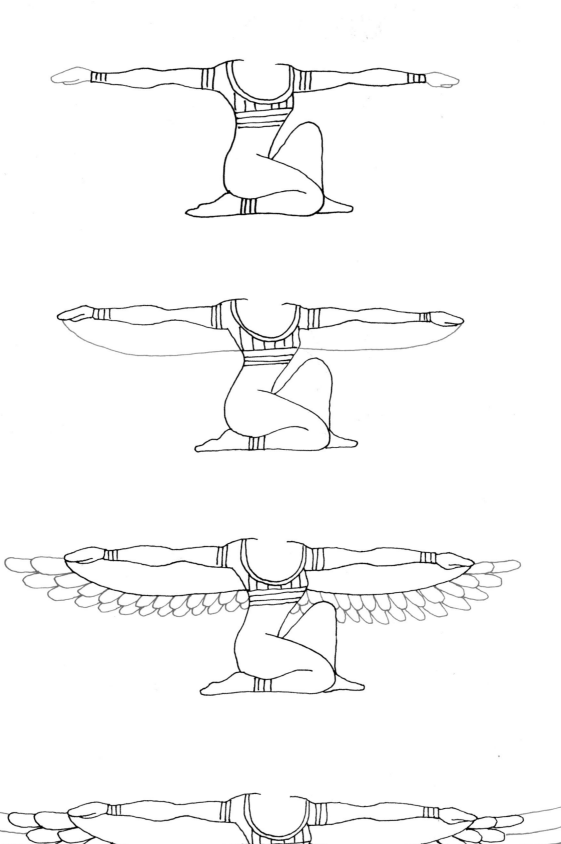

Head of Isis

Spread your wings and draw!

marker, watercolor, pastel pencil, and colored pencil

Isis was the clever and powerful goddess of the wind and the protector of motherhood. Together with the god Thoth, she taught humankind the secrets of medicine. She was also the embalmer of her slain husband, Osiris.

Queen Nefertiti

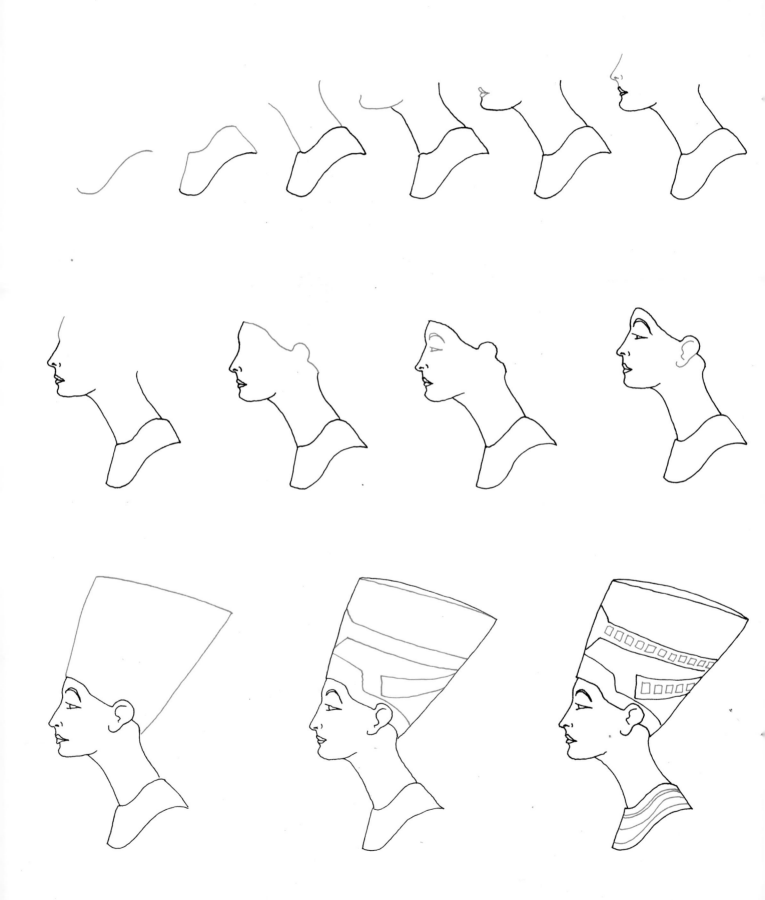

Nefertiti was a real regal beauty.

Even in ancient times Queen Nefertiti was famous for her beauty. She was married to the heretic king Akhenaten, who abandoned the traditional gods and goddesses in favor of a single god, the solar disk, Aten. During Nefertiti and Akhenaten's reign, art became more realistic and natural in appearance.

watercolor, marker, and colored pencil

Tutankhamun

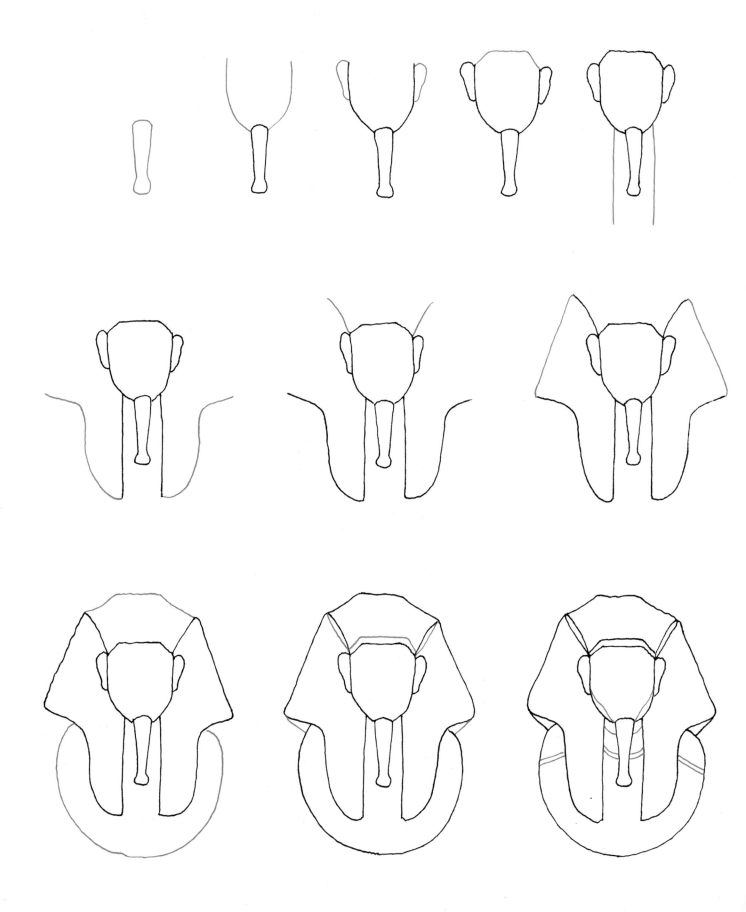

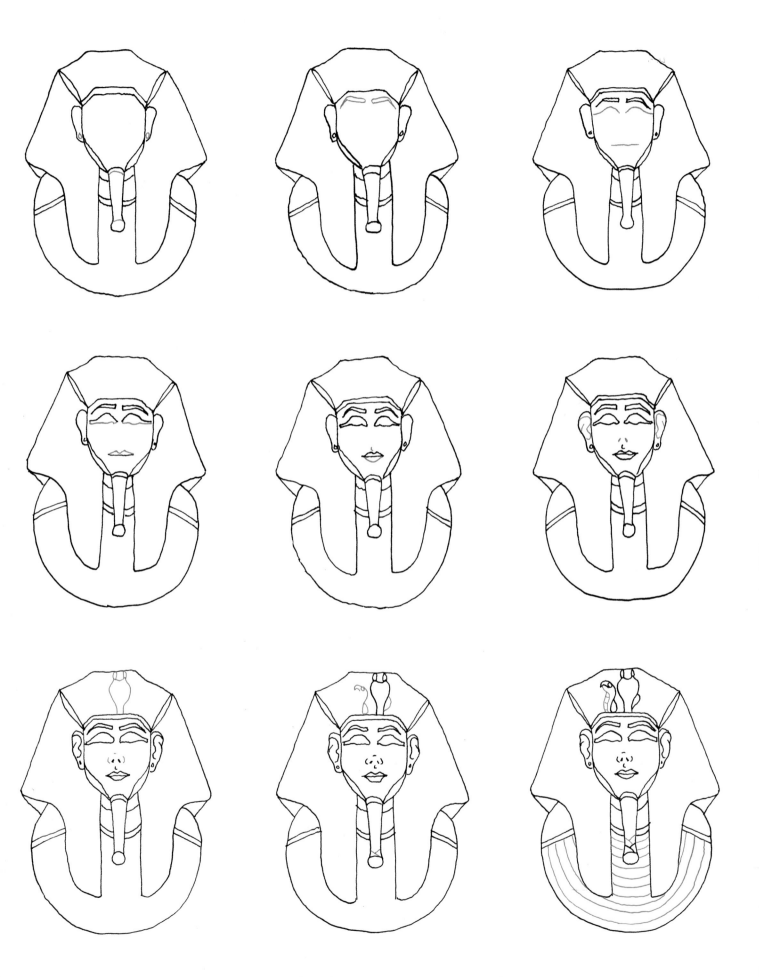

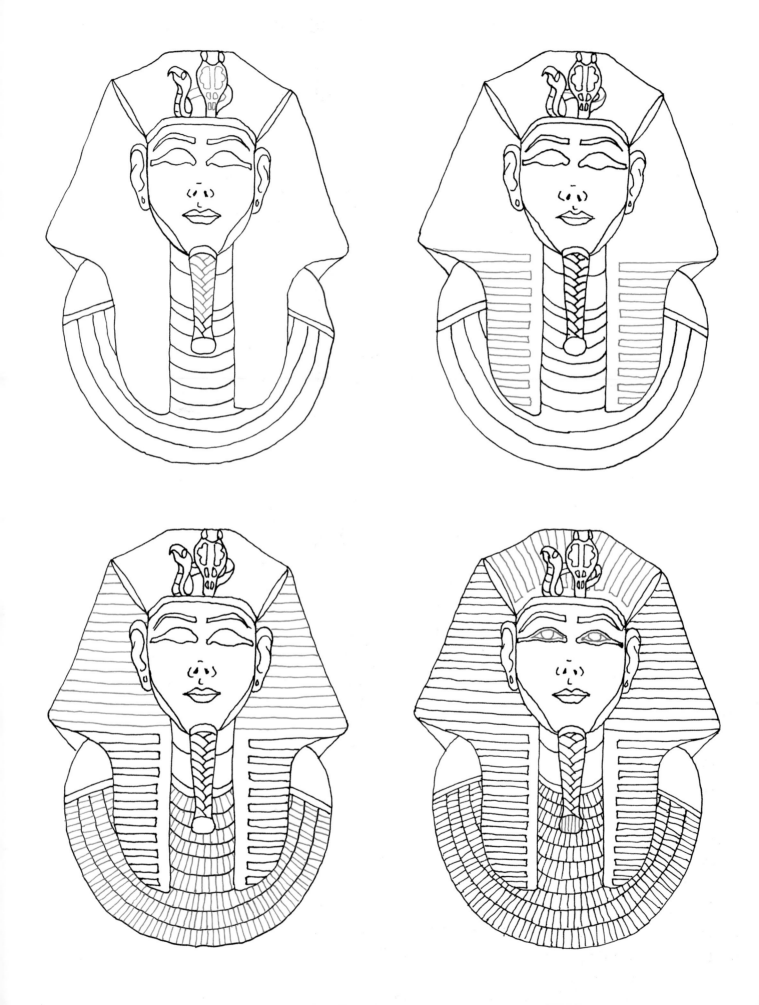

The Boy King gazes from beyond the tomb.

marker, watercolor, and colored pencil

Most likely a son of
the heretic king Akhenaten,
Tutankhamun was at birth named
Tutankhaten, meaning the "Living Image of the Aten."
He was married and became pharaoh at age nine. Two years later he restored the old
religion from before the reign of Akhenaten and changed his name to Tutankhamun,
meaning the "Living Image of Amun." King Tutankhamun died around the age of
seventeen or eighteen. His famous tomb is located in the Valley of Kings near ancient
Thebes. Smaller and less magnificent than most royal tombs, it was the most intact
when discovered by archaeologists in 1922. Some 3,500 items were recovered from his
tiny tomb, giving us a glimpse into the rich culture of Ancient Egypt.

Resources

Books for Kids

Harvey, Gill and Struan Reid. *The Usborne Internet-Linked Encyclopedia of Ancient Egypt*. Tulsa, OK: E.D.C. Publishing, 2002.

Hawass, Zahi. *Curse of the Pharaohs: My Adventures with Mummies*. Washington, D.C.: National Geographic, 2004.

Petras, Kathryn and Ross Petras. *Mummies, Gods, and Pharaohs* (Fandex Family Field Guides). New York: Workman Publishing, 2000.

Steele, Philip. *Ancient Egypt* (Curious Kids Guides). Boston: Kingfisher, 2002.

Steele, Philip. *The Best Book of Mummies*. Boston: Kingfisher, 2005.

Books for Adults

Agnese, Giorgio and Maurizio Re. *Ancient Egypt: Art and Archaeology of the Land of the Pharaohs*. New York: Barnes and Noble Books, 2000.

Muller, Hans Wolfgang. *Gold of the Pharaohs*. New York: Barnes and Noble Books, 2005.

Websites

Websites can change. Try running a search for *Ancient Egypt* on your favorite search engine.

Ancient Egypt: The Mythology
http://www.egyptianmyths.net
Use this well-organized guide to learn about Ancient Egyptian gods, goddesses, symbols, and religious beliefs.

The British Museum: Egypt
http://www.british-museum.ac.uk/world/egypt/egypt.html
Tour the largest collection of Ancient Egyptian artifacts outside of Cairo. Includes links to interactive explorations of life in Ancient Egypt.

Egyptian Museum
http://www.egyptianmuseum.gov.eg/
Explore the website of the Egyptian Museum in Cairo, which houses the largest collection of Ancient Egyptian artifacts in the world. Includes historical information as well as games.

Tour Egypt! Ancient Egypt Antiquities
http://www.touregypt.net/ancientegypt/
Find out about Ancient Egyptian history, mythology, mummies, and monuments, and convert your name into hieroglyphics. Includes a glossary and information about becoming an Egyptologist.

Pronunciation Guide

Akhenaten (ahk-NAH-tun or ah-kuh-NAH-tun)

Ammut (ah-MOOT)

Amun (AH-moon)

androsphinx (AN-druh-sfingks)

ankh (ahngk)

Anubis (uh-NOO-bus)

Aten (AH-tun)

deshret (DESH-ret)

djed (jed)

Giza (GEE-zuh)

hedjet (HEH-jet)

hieracosphinx (hye-RAH-kuh-sfingks)

Horus (HOHR-us)

Isis (EYE-sus)

Khafre (KAF-ray or KAHF-ray)

kriosphinx (KRYE-oh-sfingks)

Nefertiti (ne-fer-TEE-tee)

nekhbet (NEK-bet)

Osiris (oh-SYE-rus)

papyrus (puh-PYE-rus)

pharaoh (FER-oh, FA-roh, or FAY-roh)

pshent (puh-SHENT)

scarab (SKA-rub)

Thebes (theebz)

Tutankhamun (too-tan-KAH-mun)

Tutankhaten (too-tan-KAH-tun)

udjat (OO-jat)

uraeus (yoo-REE-us or yoo-RAY-us)